Align Your Career & Desired Lifestyle In 5 Simple Steps

by

Leanne Lindsey

Published by
LL Coaching
www.llcoaching.co.uk

Cover design: www.doubleappledesign.com
Photo: Gail D'Almaine www.dalmaine.biz

CONTENTS

INTRODUCTION

There are lots of reasons why so many of us find ourselves in careers that we do not enjoy and jobs that we hate. Most people follow the traditional education route and then get a job related to their studies. Others receive misleading careers advice or have a lack of direction after leaving education and, as a result, a part-time/temporary 'in the meantime' job becomes permanent. A lack of skills and qualifications, family commitments and financial commitments are some of the other reasons people remain in jobs that leave them feeling totally unfulfilled.

Society conditions us to stay safe, stick with what we know and avoid taking risks. As a result, many of us feel daunted, even paralysed, by the thought of change. The thought of just changing jobs is often too scary for many people, never mind changing careers altogether or going from employed to self-employed. This is the reason so many people stay in jobs that make them unhappy, and spend most of their day and night dreaming of the life they wish they had.

We are led to believe that, once we get to a certain age or take on certain responsibilities, it is time to 'grow up', and for some reason we associate that with becoming serious, risk averse and giving up on the dreams and aspirations we had in our younger days. Too often, we feel trapped by our lives and we can see no way out. We feel helpless and we resign ourselves to the fact that our lives will always be unhappy and unfulfilled. How many times have you heard someone say: "That's life" or "What can you do"?

The good news is that it is possible to align your career with your desired life.

It is possible to live a life and have a career that are fulfilling and reflect your true passions and core values. It is also possible to achieve a work/life balance. Life is precious, so we owe it to ourselves, the people around us and the world, to be happy and living a life that is truly fulfilled. The happier we are, the more joy we share with the world, and doing work that is meaningful and that matches our true passions and core values allows us to contribute to the best of our ability.

So, if you are unhappy in your current job or career, if you are feeling totally unfulfilled and uninspired by your life, if you have no work/life balance or you feel as though you are not honouring your true passions and core values, don't wait until something major happens to force you to make a change. Start the process now.

This book contains sixty-six tips from **The D.R.E.A.M Project™** that, if followed, will set you well on the way to aligning your career with your desired lifestyle and living a life that is balanced and fulfilled.

STEP 1: DETOX

The word 'detox' has become part of everyday vocabulary. It is not uncommon to hear a friend, colleague, celeb or complete stranger say they are about to start a detox, have just finished a detox or are midway through a detox. When carried out safely and responsibly, a detox can be extremely beneficial and those who embark on a detox regime notice some real physical differences, e.g. skin, hair, digestion.

What does this have to do with aligning your career with your desired lifestyle, I hear you ask?

When was the last time you looked at your emotional state and well-being?

As humans we are very good at focusing on the external, surface level stuff that the rest of the world sees. However, we are very poor at dealing with the core internal stuff that actually has more effect on the way we live our lives as well as our level of happiness and fulfilment. Too many of us spend time working on the exterior, hoping, and even believing, that if the exterior looks good the interior will take care of itself.

The fact that you are here reading this means you are experiencing some level of unhappiness or frustration. Before you can achieve balance and fulfilment in your life, it is vital that you deal with and detox the internal stuff that is causing you the discomfort and preventing you from achieving your desired lifestyle.

TIP 1: Acknowledge any negative emotions

It is really easy to go through life focusing solely on the negative things that happen and negative feelings we experience. This is especially true when we spend our days in an environment that makes us unhappy or leaves us feeling uninspired and unfulfilled. Not only does this way of life sap a huge amount of energy, it stops us from seeing all the positive things happening around us and the opportunities available to us at all times. At the same time, focusing solely on your positive emotions can also be detrimental to your health if it means you are simply ignoring your negative emotions.

Storing negative emotions and not acknowledging them can cause both mental and physical breakdown. The key is to acknowledge these negative emotions and gain some understanding as to why you are feeling this way.

TIP 2: Acknowledge your feelings towards your current job

The fact that you are reading this means it is probably your job or career that is the cause of your negative emotions. However, are you clear *exactly* what the root of the negative emotions is?

It is essential you are clear about why you are feeling uninspired or unfulfilled; otherwise, you risk making changes which actually do not bring you closer to your desired lifestyle.

Thinking about your current job, ask yourself what you enjoy and what exactly you dislike.

This will help you to identify what to look for and avoid in your next job or career. It will also help you to identify whether it is your current job or the job sector that is the issue, and whether a job move or career change is required.

TIP 3: Recognise your limiting beliefs

There may be just one or a number of reasons stopping you from living your desired lifestyle. The three most common concerns that keep people in unfulfilling and uninspiring careers are: financial commitments; lack of time; and fear of change or failure. All three concerns will be linked to what is known as a 'limiting belief'. A limiting belief is a negative emotion, and as such acts as a toxin preventing you from creating your desired lifestyle. We all have limiting beliefs, and they show up in different areas at different times in our lives.

Limiting beliefs can be paralysing, and are often the reason why people remain in situations and environments that make them unhappy.

Before you can move forward, make changes and align your career with your desired lifestyle, it is essential to identify and then dispel any limiting beliefs you have that are keeping you in a place where you are feeling unfulfilled, unhappy and uninspired.

TIP 4: Recognise your career beliefs

As well as limiting beliefs that normally affect many areas of your life you will also have career beliefs that are keeping you in a place of unhappiness and frustration. You may also have career beliefs that have helped you to become successful and achieve a lot in your career. Where you are today in your career will undoubtedly be as a result of your career beliefs.

Your career beliefs are strongly-held convictions about career choice and the world of work. These beliefs will have been formed from a very young age and will have been influenced by parents, teachers, careers advisors, peers, colleagues, society and your own personal experience. It is vital that you understand your own career beliefs and identify those that are serving you in a positive way and those that are holding you back from achieving your goals and desired lifestyle.

TIP 5: Recognise your 'time and energy vampires'

Other 'toxins' that may be stopping you from making changes are what are sometimes known as 'time and energy vampires'.

Time and energy vampires are people, activities or tasks that literally drain you and leave you feeling unmotivated and fearful, and move you away from your desired life.

Do you have someone in your life that always has something negative to say? Who always tells you why something will not work and tells you that this is just the way life is and to "get on with it"? Do you have someone in your life that tells you're too old, too young, too poor, too busy or too something else to achieve your personal goals? These people are energy vampires! Do you have regular tasks or activities that you dread doing or only do because you feel you *have* to, not because you *want* to? Are you involved in tasks or activities that go against your core values and everything you believe in? These tasks and activities are time and energy vampires!

For you, your job may actually be a major time and energy vampire. However, it could be that you have time and energy vampires in other areas of your life, and if you eliminated them you would have more time, energy and/or more money available to be able to live more aligned with your desired life.

Notes:

Before moving on to the next **D.R.E.A.M™** step, take some time to work through the questions and exercises in this step and use this page to make notes.

_____

_____

_____

_____

_____

_____

_____

_____

_____

_____

_____

_____

_____

_____

_____

_____

_____

_____

STEP 2: REFLECT

The nature of Western society is that, when we are experiencing discomfort, we either ignore it or look for a quick fix solution. It is tempting when you are feeling frustrated and unhappy in your career and life to put up with things that you are not happy with or to 'jump ship' and make rash decisions without actually taking a step back to look at things objectively and put in place a plan of action to make changes.

We live in a society where most things happen instantly and, as a consequence, many of us are very impatient. Taking time out to reflect on exactly what is causing us the discomfort and exactly what we want can seem far too time-consuming. Alternatively, taking time to look deeply at what is and isn't working for us and being honest with ourselves can be a scary prospect, and therefore many choose to keep going, living a life that is neither balanced nor fulfilled.

To align your career and your desired lifestyle, it is necessary to take time out to reflect on your life and career to date and to really think about what you want going forward.

Some people find it helpful to take a break on their own in order to really give themselves the time and space for deep reflection, without the usual everyday distractions.

TIP 6: Define your ideal life

Before making any changes to create your desired lifestyle, it is essential that you first identify *exactly* what you want that lifestyle to look like and identify any obstacles that may hold you back or get in your way. You also need to consider what help and support, if any, you will need, as well as what you are willing to compromise and/or sacrifice.

In order to create your desired lifestyle, you need clarity, and to gain clarity you need to be completely honest with yourself.

It can be a real challenge to face your fears and clearly identify your biggest dreams. However, it is essential for achieving a life of balance and fulfilment. As you know, life has a funny way of throwing obstacles in your way, particularly when you set your mind to achieve something. For this reason it is essential that you have a clear, extremely detailed vision of your ideal life.

TIP 7: Define your desired lifestyle

To align your career and desired lifestyle, you need to know what that actually means for you. It is important to be clear that, when I say desired lifestyle, I am talking about the lifestyle you would like to live that is realistic for you to achieve. For you, this could mean having more time to spend on your hobby and spending less time at work. It could be having enough money to regularly have a pamper treatment or go to the theatre. Or it could be having an income that allows you to take your children to and from school every day. It is a life that fulfils you and gives you a good work/life balance.

TIP 8: Write your career story

Many people are in their current careers through accident or circumstance; not through a clear plan they set out at the start of their working life. It could be because you left school, college or university with no clear idea of what you wanted to do or it could be due to the opportunities that were available to you at different times in your career. It is for this reason that many of us become frustrated, unfulfilled and disillusioned in our careers. Often, we don't know how we ended up where we are today or how to get to where we want to be.

Writing your career story can help you to reflect and understand the career choices you have made to date, the reasons you made them and the things that have been important to you along the way.

A well-written career story should give you a better idea of your values, talents and goals as well as a much clearer vision of the career you want going forward.

TIP 9: Define your ideal career

Once you have written your career story, you should be much clearer about what your ideal career will look like. Your career story should highlight the areas of your career you have enjoyed and would like to experience more of, as well as the things you have been tolerating and wish you could eliminate from your career for good.

Defining your ideal career gives you a clear focus and basis to start making changes in your current career. It forces you to think about what you want and how you can achieve it. Be specific about exactly what your ideal career looks like, your daily tasks, working hours, location, team, promotion prospects, etc.

TIP 10: Know your core values

Your core values provide direction and motivation, and help with decision making. Your core values are the values you hold closest to your heart and determine how you live your life.

When you are not living in alignment with your core values, you will often feel frustrated, anxious and unhappy.

It is likely that your career story will illustrate your core values and where you have made decisions that are in alignment with your core values, as well as times when you have made decisions that go against your core values and the consequences they had on your career, work/life balance and fulfilment. Honouring your core values and using them as a basis for making decisions about your life will increase your chances of success, happiness, work/life balance and fulfilment. Think of your core values as your compass on the journey of life. The fact that you are here reading this indicates that somewhere in your career you are not honouring one or more of your core values.

TIP 11: Identify your strengths

Your strengths can be described as your natural characteristics, things that you are good at and that come naturally. I am a strong believer in playing to your strengths. When you are using your strengths, you tend to have more energy and more motivation because you are able to do things well, and generally the outcome is a positive one. Identifying your strengths will help you to avoid wasting time on things that do not energise, motivate or fulfil you.

To identify your strengths, look for recurring patterns of behaviour. Consider your spontaneous reactions in different situations. Think about activities and tasks where you have consistently produced the specified outcome, as well as times when you have been able to learn quickly. In addition, think about activities and tasks you are drawn to, reflecting on what other people say you are good at.

TIP 12: Identify your skills

Skills are things you have learned to do. Many of us have a plethora of dormant skills within us that our current job role and lifestyle do not make use of. As a result, it can be easy to forget all of those useful skills we have and, more importantly, the skills that we have that we actually enjoy using. For this reason, it is essential to carry out a skills audit.

A skills audit is not an audit of the skills you are currently using; it is an audit of ALL the skills you have; all the things you have learned to do well over the years.

As well as looking at your current role, think about skills you have acquired outside your current role. Your career story can be a good place to start. Look at all of the roles you have had and identify *all* of the skills you have acquired. Consider also the skills you have gained through your previous roles, through voluntary roles, through your hobbies, interests and anything else you do outside of your current job role. Once you have completed your skills audit, go through all your skills and highlight those you actually enjoy using.

TIP 13: Identify your interests

If you are interested in the work you do, the chances are that you will enjoy it. Therefore, it is important to identify your interests.

Knowing what your interests are will give you a good reference point when considering the work you do as well as the things you would like to incorporate into your desired lifestyle.

When identifying your interests, think beyond your hobbies. Also, consider any causes, issues and campaigns that you are passionate about or interested in. Think about the books and magazines you read, the programmes and films you watch and the types of holidays you enjoy.

TIP 14: Identify your career likes and dislikes

As well as considering your strengths, skills and interests, it is also important to think about the aspects of your career you like and the aspects of your career you dislike. In the same way it is important to be in a role that plays to your strengths, it is also important for your career to incorporate more of the things you like than the things you dislike. As mentioned in the Detox section, things that you do not like act as energy vampires and will leave you feeling demotivated. Think about the aspects of your career you have consistently enjoyed over the years; the things that you yearn to do more of and would happily do for years to come. Also, consider the aspects that you wouldn't miss and would quite happily eliminate from your career.

TIP 15: Identify your personal likes and dislikes

In addition to identifying the aspects of your career that you like and dislike, it is also useful to think about your personal everyday likes and dislikes.

What things energise you and leave you wanting more, and what things do you avoid like the plague?

Of course, all jobs will involve tasks and aspects that we don't necessarily enjoy. However, if you can identify exactly what you like and dislike, it will enable you to steer your career in the direction of roles that consist more of what you like than what you dislike. As a result, you should have more energy to do more of what you like and enjoy, in alignment with your desired lifestyle.

TIP 16: Identify your preferred working style

It is important to recognise your preferred working style. If you prefer working on your own but you are working in a large team, then of course you will feel frustration and anxiety on a daily basis. If you prefer to work independently but you have a supervisor, manager or team leader who insists you report to them on every task you are working on, again you will feel frustration and resentment on a regular basis.

Thinking about your current and previous roles, identify the aspects of the working style required that frustrated you. Then, think about the working styles that totally worked for you and where you felt at ease to be yourself while still being effective and productive.

TIP 17: Define your ideal working environment

This is similar to your preferred working style. However, it is looking more at the physical environment. Do you prefer to work in the office or from home? Do you prefer an office with natural light? Do you prefer an open office or small project rooms? Do you prefer to be close to shops or surrounded by nature? Do you prefer to work in a large organisation or a small business? Again, thinking about your current and previous job roles, what have you loved about your working environments? What have you missed when moving from one job role to another? Many of us spend more time at work than we do in our own homes. Therefore, it is important to be in an environment that we feel comfortable in.

TIP 18: Find your passion

"Find something you love to do and you'll never have to work a day in your life."

This is true to some extent. However, many other factors are considered when choosing a career, in particular, the lifestyle we wish to live. However, what tends to happen to many people is that they end up in a career they do not enjoy and with a lifestyle that leaves them feeling totally unfulfilled.

Finding your passion increases your chances of experiencing happiness, balance and fulfilment on a regular basis.

Once you know where your passion lies, you are more able to identify opportunities for aligning your career with your passion, resulting in a life that is balanced and fulfilled.

Your passion can be described as: something you truly enjoy doing; something you can do for hours without getting bored; something you yearn to do when you are not doing it; and something that leaves you feeling energised and fulfilled. Your passion gives you a purpose, motivates you, adds meaning to your life, and gives you direction. In order to align your career with your desired lifestyle, it is vital that you know what your passion is. It is impossible to achieve your desired lifestyle if you do not know where your passion lies. Make a list of all the things you absolutely love to do, the things that get your heart racing just thinking about them, and the things that you would happily do even if you were not getting paid.

Notes:

Before moving onto the next **D.R.E.A.M™** step, take some time to work through the questions and exercises in this step and use this page to make notes.

_____

_____

_____

_____

_____

_____

_____

_____

_____

_____

_____

_____

_____

_____

_____

_____

_____

STEP 3: EXPLORE

Now that you have had time to reflect and identify your strengths, skills and interests, you should have a clearer vision of what you would like your desired life to look like.

It should now be clear whether or not your job and career are aligned with your desired lifestyle.

The next stage is to explore the opportunities available that will enable you to align your career more closely with your vision of your desired lifestyle.

Remember, the options listed in this section are not a finite list; they are the most common ones considered and the ones that are most readily available to many of you.

TIP 19: Same job role, same company, same industry

The first and easiest option is to remain in your current job role and to identify any opportunities to improve things or make changes in your current position.

Pinpoint what is causing the negative feelings you have about your job. Look at your own attitude, and honestly assess whether your own attitude is affecting your happiness and fulfilment. Think about whether any changes can be made to the projects/tasks you work on, the way you work or to your working arrangements. Think about what initially attracted you to the job, the company and the industry. Ask yourself what has changed and how you can reignite those feelings.

TIP 20: Different job role, same company, same industry

Look out for any new opportunities that may be available. Think outside of your current job role and responsibilities, and consider opportunities both within your department and other departments. Speak to people currently doing job roles you are interested in to find out exactly what the role involves. Speak to people in other departments, not only to find out what opportunities are available but also to express your interest.

TIP 21: Same job role, different company, same industry

You may find that you love your job and enjoy working in the industry but decide that you absolutely cannot continue to work for your current company. It could be that your values do not align with the company's values or it could be that the remuneration is inadequate. Before you make that decision, however, identify exactly what it is that you do not like about the company you currently work for. Identify exactly what is causing you to feel unhappy, frustrated or unfulfilled in your current company.

TIP 22: Different job role, different company, same industry

It might be that you have a real interest in the industry you currently work in but you are not happy in your job role and company. Identify exactly what it is that you do not like about your current job role. Identify exactly what it is that you do not like about the company you currently work for. Look at your core values and what is important to you about the company you currently work for, and identify companies that reflect this.

TIP 23: Same job role, different company, different industry

You may discover that you actually do like the job you are currently doing. However, you have no interest in the industry you are currently working in, and as a result you also dislike the company you are working for. Identify exactly what it is that you do not like about the industry you currently work in. Also, look at exactly what you dislike about the company you currently work for.

What exactly is causing you to feel unhappy, frustrated or unfulfilled?

Look at your core values, interests and any causes you feel strongly about and identify industries that reflect these.

TIP 24: Different job role, different company, different industry

After exploring all of the options mentioned above, it may become clear that a complete career change is the only solution that will enable you to align your career with your desired lifestyle. Look at the answers to all the questions you have answered so far. Think about your core values, interests, talents, strengths, skills and any causes you feel strongly about, and identify all the industries and job roles that match these. Consider a transitional approach, selecting one of the options above, changing one thing at a time.

TIP 25: Volunteer for a cause you are passionate about

As well as the options already discussed, there are other options that you can consider. Voluntary work can be beneficial, no matter what stage you are at. It enables you to help a cause you are passionate about and to do work that reflects your core values and interests. Volunteering can help you to increase your skills, allow you to use more of the skills you enjoy using, and learn new skills. It can give you the opportunity to gain experience in and knowledge of a new role or career path. Additionally, volunteering can give you an insight into how other companies operate.

TIP 26: Invest in your personal development and training

Most of us live in a fast-paced, ever changing society and, in order to compete and stay relevant, we must continue to grow. In order to do this, it is vital that you invest time, money and energy into your own personal growth.

Whether you decide to stay in your current role or you choose to change role, company, industry or career, training can enhance your current skills and knowledge.

Consequently, training may increase your chances of promotion, improve your employability and ease your transition. On a personal level, it is essential to keep working on yourself, as life can be challenging and demanding and, the more work you do on yourself, the better equipped you will be to make decisions that will align your core values and true passions in all areas of your life.

TIP 27: Become a freelancer or contractor

In some industries, freelancing and contracting are common ways of working. They offer flexibility and tend to pay more than employed work.

Freelancing and contracting give you much more freedom to choose where, when and how you work, and for how long.

They can offer a lot of variety in your work as well as give you an insight into many more companies and industries. There is, of course, more financial risk and less security with freelancing and contracting, and careful consideration must be taken before deciding to follow this option. It is essential that you do your research, seek advice from professionals and assess all the risks involved.

TIP 28: Consider a portfolio career

With a portfolio career, generally you would have a full-time job and a part-time job or two, or more part-time jobs. The idea is that you get to use a variety of skills, strengths and interests. Like freelancing and contracting, having a portfolio career can offer a lot of variety in your work as well as give you an insight into several companies and industries. A portfolio career can also be a stepping stone to starting your own business and can act as supplementary income.

TIP 29: Set up your own business

Many people have a dream of one day being their own boss, and this could be a valid option for you if you have a specific talent or skill, if you have idea for a new or improved product or service or if you have identified a gap in a particular market.

Running your own business can be extremely rewarding. However, it also comes with huge risks, and the decision to start your own business must not be taken lightly.

As with freelancing and contracting, it is essential that you do your research, seek advice from professionals and business owners, and assess all the risks involved.

TIP 30: Move, work abroad or emigrate

Sometimes, it is easy to forget that the world we live in is huge, and we do not consider the opportunities that are available in other cities, let alone other countries. Of course, there are so many more things that need to be considered before making a decision to move city, town or county, and even more when considering working abroad or emigrating. This does not mean it is impossible and, depending on your circumstances, it may be a viable option for you. Again, do your research to find out what opportunities are available, and exactly what is involved, as every country will have its own laws and policies on working and emigrating. Also, speak to anyone you know that has experience of moving, working or emigrating abroad.

TIP 31: Downsize your life

Another option you have is to downsize your life. This generally means reducing your financial outgoings and commitments, which can give you more freedom to choose the way you work. The idea being that, the lower your outgoings, the less you need to earn, and therefore the less you need to work; giving you more time to do the things you love and enjoy. In modern society many of us have lives filled with 'stuff', and normally stuff we don't actually want, use or need. Freeing ourselves of this need to fill our lives with stuff we don't want or need may actually give us the space and freedom to fill our lives with stuff we actually want and need.

Notes:

Before moving onto the next **D.R.E.A.M™** step, take some time to work through the questions and exercises in this step and use this page to make notes.

_____

_____

_____

STEP 4: ACTION

Having a clear vision of your desired life is great and should initially make you feel motivated and give you hope that things can improve significantly. However, if you do not start taking immediate action towards making your desired lifestyle a reality, you will lose momentum and your motivation, and before too long you will probably start to feel even more frustrated than you did previously. This is because you are now much clearer about what you want, you now know how you can achieve what you want, but nothing is happening.

The only real way for you to align your career with your desired lifestyle is to take action.

TIP 32: Create an action plan

After working through the Detox, Reflect and Explore sections above, the overall goal of aligning your career and desired lifestyle may seem huge, and may leave you feeling overwhelmed. This is why it is important to break up your overall goal into much smaller steps, and an action plan is a great way of doing that. Your action plan will outline the smaller steps you need to take in order to achieve your larger goal. The steps outlined in your action plan should be SMART: Specific, Measurable, Achievable, Realistic and Time-Bound.

Your action plan should contain a mixture of short-term, relatively easy-to-achieve action steps, as well as longer-term action steps that will stretch you and take you out of your comfort zone. As your action plan will clearly show the steps you need to take, and by when, it will help you to hold yourself accountable and will highlight any areas of hesitation and avoidance. Use this book as a basis for your action plan, especially if you have read this far but haven't completed any of the exercises. Think about all the things you will need to do and all the people you will need to speak to in order to achieve your overall goal of aligning your career with your desired lifestyle. Plan how long each step will take you, decide when you will do each step, and then schedule the time into your diary. It is very important that you schedule your action steps and deadlines into your diary otherwise life can get in the way and, before you know it, six months have passed and you are no closer to achieving your goal. Additionally, integrating your action plan with your diary demonstrates your commitment to achieving your goal, as it means you are making it a priority in your life.

If you do not have a diary – either paper, online or on your phone/handheld device – GET ONE!

TIP 33: Carry out a risk assessment

When creating your action plan, you should also include a risk assessment. More often than not in life, achieving something worthwhile involves some risk, and, generally, the bigger the achievement, the higher the level of risk it will involve. Risk taking can be the one thing that stands in the way of a person and their goal, either because they become paralysed through fear of the level of risk involved or because they take the risk without calculating and appreciating the level involved. For this reason, it is essential that you calculate the level of risk involved with any decisions you make and any actions you take to align your career and your desired lifestyle.

Once you have identified the risk involved, you can then work out a contingency plan, just in case the worst case scenario does happen. Identifying the level of risk involved and devising a contingency plan will make the decisions you make feel less scary. As part of your risk assessment you should look at personal risks, financial risks and risks to others.

TIP 34: Get organised

Now that you have an action plan and a contingency plan, before doing anything else you must get organised. Even if you are a person who works better in chaos and clutter, you will give yourself a much better chance of achieving your goal if you get organised from the outset. Your career is only one aspect of your life, which means it is almost certain that you will have other demands on your time outside of achieving your goal. Being organised will help you to manage these demands more effectively and will help you to be proactive rather than reactive when conflicts between the demands of everyday life and achieving your goal occur. Make a list of all the demands on your time, and ensure you include the things you like to do as well as the things you feel you *have* to do. Include small demands such as feeding the cat or dog as well as bigger demands such as taking the children to a weekly activity.

TIP 35: Review your finances

Money is often the primary concern for most people, and is usually the first thing people say is standing between where they are today and where they want to be in the future. It is also something many people mismanage or avoid thinking about.

In order to align your career and your desired lifestyle, money is something you absolutely must review and manage effectively.

Identify your weekly, monthly, quarterly and annual outgoings. Remember to include the smaller things such lunch, newspapers, magazines, coffees, travel, as well as the bigger, less regular things such as car breakdown cover, annual holidays and spending money, birthday and Christmas presents, etc. Work out your savings, and calculate how much you need to put aside for emergencies. Additionally, if you already have considerable savings, consider how much, if any, you want to use to move you closer to your desired lifestyle. Once you have clearly identified your outgoings and savings, identify any opportunities for 'cutting costs' and reducing your outgoings, potentially giving you more disposable income to assist you with creating your desired lifestyle.

TIP 36: Create a vision board

A vision board is a collection of images that visually represents your goal, dream or ambition. It can be used to constantly remind you what you are working towards and, because it is visual, it can make it easier to believe that it is achievable. Create a vision board that reflects what you have defined as your desired lifestyle. Make it as detailed as possible, and include photos, quotes and any important dates or values. It should reflect not only your desired lifestyle but also what your career needs to look like in order to achieve it. Put your vision board somewhere you will see it every day.

TIP 37: Write a vision statement

A vision statement is a statement of intent, detailing what you want to achieve.

Having a vision statement gives you clarity by clearly defining a purpose and priorities.

Ensure you quantify anything you can. Make it measurable. Write it succinctly in a number of measurable elements – ten is a recommended number. Be as clear and precise as possible. Keep your vision statement somewhere you will see it every day. It could even form part of your vision board.

For most of you reading this, aligning your career with your desired lifestyle is a huge challenge. There is a reason you are here reading this and a reason why you have not achieved it thus far. It is not because you are a failure, or even because you are lazy; it is more likely to be because you have not had the right support to keep you encouraged, motivated and focused.

Society tells us that it is normal to feel unhappy and unfulfilled, and that this is the way life is. That it is normal to work extremely long hours, have little or no work/life balance and even less time for fun, relaxation and time with family and friends. Many people have resigned themselves to this view of society and either do not believe there is another way, do not have the energy to even attempt another way or are too scared to try another way. Many of these people may be your own friends or family. This means you may find that, when you set out on your journey to align your career and your desired lifestyle, you may actually receive more negative views than positive support.

It can be very useful to get yourself a coach or a mentor.

A coach or mentor is someone who will support and encourage you but will also hold you accountable. A mentor is generally someone who has already achieved success at whatever it is you are setting out to achieve, whereas a coach may not necessarily have achieved the same goal as you. However, they are trained to help you reach your full potential, no matter what your goal is.

It may be that you do have a supportive network of friends and family, and if that is the case then do tap into them and share your journey with them. However, friends and family will generally offer advice based on their own experiences, fears, values and beliefs, so it is still useful to have someone neutral, who does not know you personally and who can support you objectively.

TIP 39: Talk to others

When embarking on a goal such as aligning your career with your desired lifestyle, it can be a daunting, overwhelming and sometimes lonely journey. There will be times when you come up against unforeseen obstacles and challenges, and times when you will feel like you are the only person in the world going through this. You may even feel like giving up. This is why it is important to speak to other people who have already achieved the goal you are working towards. This can be talking to actual people or it can be through reading books and watching interviews with/documentaries about people. The Internet has unlimited resources for any subject you choose to research. Online forums can be very informative and often have people who will answer questions you post. Find online forums for people who are considering a career change or are looking to achieve a better work/life balance. You may not even need to post your question; just reading the responses and progress of others may be all the encouragement you need to keep working towards achieving your goal.

TIP 40: Get your CV reviewed and updated by a professional

Whatever you decide to do next, it is likely that you will need to have an up to date CV. Most of us will spend hours updating our CV, never really feeling confident that the format, length and content actually fit what a potential employer is looking for. How many of us were actually shown how to write a professional CV? Most of us were shown how to do a basic CV when we were leaving school or university, with little or no work experience to include. Therefore, it is almost certain that the format we were taught then is not actually the format that is expected by most employers today.

Many of us then learn to write a CV through trial and error, from feedback from employers and agencies or we just copy the format of a friend or colleague we know has been successful in their career. This may have worked for you in the past. However, the job market has changed tremendously and has become fiercely competitive.

To stand a chance of being offered an interview, you must ensure your CV stands out from the crowd and catches the employer's eye.

A professional CV writer will not only ensure that the format of your CV is desirable to employers; a good, professional CV writer will also work with you to articulate your career goals and achievements, your core skills and strengths and relevant work experience, concisely using optimised keywords and phrases. Having a professionally written CV can increase your chances of being offered an interview as well as lessen the anxiety of not knowing whether your CV is the issue when receiving all the "thanks but no thanks" letters, or worst still, no response at all. There are numerous companies offering CV writing services. Do your research, speak to them, and ask them exactly what service you can expect to receive, what results they have helped clients achieve in the past, whether they have testimonials from previous clients and what guarantee, if any, they offer.

Love it or hate it, social media is very much a part of life as we know it today. There are a number of social media sites, the most popular currently being Facebook, Twitter and LinkedIn. An online profile gives you the opportunity to showcase your strengths, skills, interests and experience to potential employers, and can increase your visibility and credibility in your current field or the field you wish to move into.

An online profile gives you the opportunity to network, share your knowledge and develop and maintain relationships.

Twitter can help you to get to know new people, whereas Facebook is generally used to develop and maintain existing relationships, more commonly with friends, family and colleagues. Facebook is also used by many to develop business relationships and networks. LinkedIn is used to maintain a network of colleagues and business contacts that you already know or have had some interaction with. It is also now increasingly used by potential employers to identify suitable candidates for vacancies.

LinkedIn is recognised as the portal to use for professional networking and as such it is recommended that you create a LinkedIn profile if you do not already have one. Remember, your online profile is a reflection of who you are as a professional, and you need to ensure it paints an accurate picture. Make sure you have a professional photo – not one of you on holiday or on a night out partying, unless of course that reflects who you are as a professional. Complete all sections of your profile in as much detail as possible; again, your career story should help you with this.

Finally, join any groups that reflect where you want to be. So, if you want to remain in your current field, join groups within that field and regularly comment on group discussions. If you want to change career, join groups in the industry you want to move into, and use the information shared to increase your knowledge and, when you are able to make informed, constructive comments, start to contribute to the groups.

It is important to state that anything you include in your online profile is potentially accessible by anyone, and, as such, ensure that you only include information that you are happy to share publicly.

TIP 42: Update your online profile

You may have already joined the social media revolution and have one or more online profiles.

Are your online profiles consistent with the professional image you wish to reflect?

If you have a Facebook account, what comments do you make? What photos do you have on there? Are they comments and photos that reflect you in the best professional light? If not, then it is time to update your profile. You may be thinking that your Facebook profile is private and nothing to do with your career and professional image. However, the nature of online information is that you never really know who can access it, and employers are now looking at the online profiles of potential candidates.

If you already have a LinkedIn account, it is essential that your profile is fully up to date and accurately reflects your skills, strengths and experience. Your profile should have a good photo and testimonials from people you have worked with. You should have joined a number of relevant groups and you should be contributing to group discussions on a regular basis.

Twitter is not essential but can be useful for keeping up to date with current issues and topics you are interested in. If you already have a Twitter account, ensure you are not tweeting about irrelevant things such as what you ate for dinner last night. Remember, your tweets are available for anyone to read, and you never know who may be reading them.

TIP 43: Define your personal brand

Your personal brand is how you market yourself to others – both consciously and subconsciously – and, as such, determines how you are perceived by others. You may think this sounds quite conceited, but the truth is that people make up their minds about you based on what they see in the first few seconds. They judge you based on how you are dressed, what you say and how you behave. Whether you think this is right or wrong, the bottom line is that this is the way the human race works. Be honest, what do you do when you meet someone for the first time? For this reason, it is important to be clear exactly how you want to be perceived by people and, once you are clear, you can ensure your actions and appearance are consistent with this.

Put simply, your personal brand ensures the way you see yourself is aligned with the way other people perceive you.

You have already considered most of the elements that make up your personal brand in the Reflect section. Your passion, interests, core values and the strengths and skills you enjoy using are all part of your personal brand. In addition, your online profile and your personal style are vital elements of your personal brand. Consider how you see yourself, how others perceive you, and identify any inconsistencies.

TIP 44: Write an 'elevator pitch'

Now that you have defined your personal brand, you need to write an 'elevator pitch'. Once someone has met or seen you for the first time and made their judgements based on how you look, the next thing they will make a judgment on is what you say.

It essential that what you say reflects your personal brand.

Opportunities are all around us. All the time, however, many of us miss these opportunities because we are unclear about who we are and what we want, and are therefore unable to articulate this to others. You meet people all the time either through traditional networking or just a person you meet in a coffee shop, at a seminar or while waiting in a queue. These are potential opportunities that may move you closer to your goal of aligning your career with your desired lifestyle.

An elevator pitch is an introduction or short summary that defines who you are, what you are looking for and what you can offer. It should take no longer than sixty seconds to deliver; the idea being that, if you met someone in an elevator with the opportunity of a lifetime, you are able to sell yourself to them before they leave the elevator. Your elevator pitch needs to be clear and concise. It needs to create urgency and necessity that compels the listener to take immediate action. Keep it simple – no more than three key points – and make it personal. Remember the harsh reality is that no one cares about you and your story; they care about what you can do for them and how can you help them. They want to know what benefits you can offer.

TIP 45: Keep an ideas book and journal

I am sure that, while reading this, many thoughts and ideas have come to mind. You may have made notes in the Notes sections of this book, in a separate notebook or even on a scrap of paper. This is just the beginning of the process. You are embarking on a potentially long and challenging journey, and you will experience a range of emotions and will also almost certainly have an abundance of ideas flowing in and out of your mind during the journey.

For most of us, our minds are constantly occupied with thoughts of what we still have to do and what we didn't get around to doing, as well as being bombarded with external stimuli. Our minds are already occupied with so much that it can be normal to forget things from time to time. But what if that thing you have forgotten is a strategy for moving jobs? Or an organisation you thought it might be useful to contact? This is where an ideas book and journal can be very useful. It can be used to store any ideas and thoughts you have, as well as to express any emotions that you don't feel able to share with others. It can also help you to make sense of your emotions and removes the stress of trying to remember 101 things as well as the pressure not to forget anything. It is not uncommon to have your best ideas at the most inconvenient time. Having an ideas book and journal allows you to store the idea and to come back to it when you have more time.

Keep your journal with you at all times.

Notes:

Before moving onto the next **D.R.E.A.M™** step, take some time to work through the questions and exercises in this step and use this page to make notes.

_____

_____

_____

_____

_____

_____

_____

_____

_____

_____

_____

_____

_____

_____

_____

_____

_____

STEP 5: MAKEOVER

Now that you have an action plan, you are ready to start working towards aligning your career and desired lifestyle, creating a life that is balanced and fulfilled. However, having an action plan alone will not get you through the challenging times that are sure to come. You will certainly experience many breakthroughs; however, you are also certain to experience a few breakdowns along the way.

To maximise your chances of success, you will need to start making changes to your lifestyle from the beginning.

You will also need to ensure that your mindset is one of success and in a state that will give you the best possible chance of achieving your goal.

TIP 46: Review your daily routine

Despite reading this far, having a clear vision and goal, along with an action plan and contingency plan, your everyday life will carry on as it always did before reading this. You will no doubt already have several demands on your time as well as commitments and obligations that you must still honour, and these will not disappear just because you have made a commitment to make changes in your life. When you first make the commitment, your motivation and dedication will be strong. However, after a few setbacks or missed deadlines, the temptation to give up will become stronger.

As with most things in life, prevention is better than a cure. You know that life will go on. However, you now have another commitment to honour: a commitment to yourself to achieve your desired lifestyle and to live a life that is balanced and fulfilled. You will, no doubt, have times when you are not being very productive, and may actually be wasting your time on things that are moving you away from your desired lifestyle, rather than moving you closer to it.

Write down your daily routine; a typical day in your life. If each day varies significantly, do this for a whole week. Once you have done so, review your routine and identify time slots that you could be using more productively to work on your action steps for aligning your career and desired lifestyle, and start to schedule slots where you will work on your action steps.

TIP 47: Take a break

Once you have reviewed your routine, it is important to remember to include time to rest and time to have fun. When working towards a goal, it can be very tempting to focus solely on that goal until you have achieved it – at the expense of other things that matter in your life. Regularly taking a break gives you the opportunity not only to rest but also to reflect on your progress, to acknowledge your achievements and to identify areas for further development. Taking a break can help you to regain clarity and to ensure that the goal you are working towards is still one that you want, and that you are still on track.

Rest is essential, as it allows the body and mind to recover from the stresses of everyday life. During this time, the mind has the opportunity to expand, and it is often the time when people feel the most inspired.

TIP 48: Maintain your health

Good health is something that we all know is integral to a long and happy life, yet many of us take it for granted and do not value it until we no longer have it or are at risk of losing it. Working towards a goal such as aligning your career with your desired lifestyle can be quite intense and, often, when we are short on time, money and/or energy, one of the first things to be sacrificed is our health. Many of us believe our health will take care of itself and we prioritise many other things before taking care of ourselves. However, it is important to remember that without good health it is almost impossible to enjoy any other area of life. What is the point of aligning your career and desired lifestyle if you are too ill to enjoy the lifestyle you have created?

It is essential that, no matter how focused you are on your goal, you make time to maintain your health.

Exercise regularly, even if that is just a daily walk around the local park or dancing around your living room, and eat well. Food is fuel for the body, and without it you will not have the energy to enjoy the lifestyle you have created. Maintaining good health should be integral to the lifestyle you are working towards.

TIP 49: Be kind to yourself

During the journey of aligning your career with your desired lifestyle, there will be many ups and downs. Some people go through life focusing on the downside to everything and never acknowledging the positives. Likewise, when working towards something, some people will focus on and be deeply affected by any obstacles or setbacks they encounter, but will never stop to acknowledge their achievements. On a journey such as this one, it is essential to take time to reflect on and acknowledge your achievements. There will be challenging times, and there may even be people around you who doubt or question you. Therefore, you must be your biggest cheerleader and be kind to yourself.

Acknowledge the progress you have made, no matter how small it may be.

Use your journal to note any significant achievements so that you can remind yourself at times when you are feeling challenged.

TIP 50: Accept that change is inevitable

Change is inevitable, so it makes sense to accept change rather than resist it. The fact that you are here reading this means that you probably want something to change in your life. However, wanting changes in your life does not necessarily mean you will be comfortable with the changes that will occur along the way. In fact, many people fear and resist change and therefore remain unhappy and unfulfilled.

It is important that you accept that change is inevitable no matter what you decide to do in life.

Even if you decide not to change, the world around you will change, with or without you. The nature of aligning your career with your desired lifestyle will involve a multitude of changes, and the overall goal is to change the way your life is today, so it is essential you learn to accept that change is inevitable and part of the journey.

TIP 51: Embrace failure

Many people who feel unhappy and unfulfilled actually have fantastic plans and ideas of how they can live happier, more fulfilled lives. However, most of them make no attempt to see these plans and ideas through because they are too scared they might fail. What you absolutely must understand and accept is that 'failure' is a part of life.

Anyone who has ever achieved anything big or small has undoubtedly failed along the way.

This may sound clichéd but it is true to say that there is no such thing as failure; just lessons to be learned about what works and what doesn't work. Thomas Edison famously said about his invention of the light bulb: "I have not failed. I've just found 10,000 ways that won't work." What would life be like now if Thomas Edison had quit after attempt 1,000 or even attempt 9,999?

We learn more from our failures than we do from our successes, and for this reason it is important to embrace failure and any obstacles you encounter as they are opportunities to grow and to learn how to do things better. Remember, almost all obstacles and setbacks are temporary, no matter how permanent they appear to be at the time. Focus on the learning to be taken from the situation and get back on track as soon as possible.

TIP 52: Understand FEAR

FEAR is often referred to as False Evidence Appearing Real. This is very true. Fear is not fact. It is based on the assumption that something may or may not happen. However, when people are operating from a state of fear they very rarely consider the alternative option. They very rarely consider the positive outcomes that are actually just as probable as the negative outcomes they are dreading.

Fear will never go away. It's a natural human instinct, and it is actually there to protect us from danger. Fear has a very valid purpose in life and can be essential to our survival. If we suddenly came face to face with a lion, fear would kick in and trigger our survival 'fight or flight' mode. Over the centuries, society has conditioned us to fear regular, everyday situations that we find uncomfortable or challenging in the same way. However, how often are we actually faced with a real life or death situation? Fear will paralyse you, so it is absolutely paramount to your success that you are able to recognise and understand fear for what it is and keep moving towards your goal regardless of what may or may not happen. As long as you have carried out your research and risk assessment, you have to just 'feel the fear' and do it anyway!

TIP 53: Choose your thoughts carefully

Thoughts are extremely powerful, and it is a common belief that what you think you become. The thoughts we think have a direct impact on our emotions and attitudes, and this in turn affects the choices and decisions we make in life. If you are a person that has a negative outlook, I am guessing that negative stuff regularly happens in your life. Likewise, if you are a person that maintains a positive outlook, I'm guessing that on the whole positive things regularly happen in your life.

Having a positive outlook on life will increase your chances of achieving your goal of aligning your career with your desired lifestyle.

Having a positive mindset will also help you to better deal with and manage any obstacles or challenges you may encounter. Pay attention to your thoughts, and start to become more conscious of the thoughts you have daily. Are they positive or negative? Are they thoughts of success or of failure? Also, identify the source of your thoughts. What triggers them and where have they come from? Are they the thoughts of others that you have absorbed or are they your own? We have the ability to choose our thoughts, so choose them well! Ensure the thoughts you are having on a regular basis are encouraging and are supporting you to move closer to your goal.

TIP 54: Count your blessings

There will be times, of course, when no amount of positive thinking and self-belief will help you to feel better about an obstacle or setback. During these times, it is important to have an 'attitude of gratitude' and think about all the good things you have in your life, all the things you have achieved and, essentially, all the things you have to be grateful for. When faced with adversity, it is very tempting to go into 'victim' mode and think about all the things that have gone wrong, all the things that are not working and all the things you do not have. No matter how bad things are, it is very rare that life is as bad as you are feeling.

On a very basic level, if you have shelter and food, then already you have something to be grateful for. If you have friends and family, a job, regular income and a car, then you have plenty to be grateful for. When you are feeling stuck, down or frustrated, take some time to reflect on the progress you have made as well as making a list of everything you have to be grateful for – big and small.

TIP 55: Believe in yourself

If you don't believe in yourself, why should anyone else?

Self-belief is a vital component of achieving success.

When you encounter your challenges, obstacles and setbacks, self-belief can be one of the first things to waiver. However, it is your self-belief that will keep you moving towards your goal. When everyone around you doubts you, again it is your own self-belief that will carry you through and will support you in achieving your goal of aligning your career with your desired lifestyle.

Many of us regularly offer words of support and encouragement to friends, family, colleagues and even perfect strangers because we are able to see their true potential and all the possibilities available to them. However, we often struggle to see the same for ourselves. No matter how much belief someone else has in you, if you do not believe in yourself, no amount of belief from someone else will matter in the long term.

Remember, your goal is personal to you, as is your vision for your life. Therefore, only you know the true value it holds for you. Regularly reflect on your core strengths, skills and achievements in order to keep in mind how capable you are of achieving your goal.

TIP 56: Be committed

It is not enough to have an action plan and believe in yourself.

You must also be 100% committed to achieving your goal of aligning your career with your desire lifestyle.

Without this commitment, it will be extremely challenging to achieve your goal, especially when faced with obstacles and setbacks. Along with your self-belief, it is your commitment that will keep you motivated and will give you the strength to keep going even when you feel like giving up completely.

How often in life have you said you want something – and maybe even said you'll do whatever it takes to get it – but then, when told how to achieve it, you do nothing? Many of us want a guarantee of success before we will fully commit to something. However, life does not come with guarantees. If you want to achieve your desired lifestyle the answer is simple: commit to it and put in the work.

TIP 57: Take responsibility

Many people go through life blaming others for things they haven't achieved, things they don't have and generally their overall unhappiness or lack of fulfilment with their life. Some blame the government; others blame their parents. Some blame their education or lack of it, some blame their boss or the organisation they work for, and some people blame all of these things.

When you blame others you are not taking responsibility for your life or your desired outcomes.

You are essentially putting the immense power you have to achieve your desired lifestyle into someone else's hands. You are allowing others to control your life and the direction it takes, which results in frustration and unhappiness. Of course, your friends, your family, your manager, the government, etc. can influence the decisions you make. However, you must understand that you are ultimately responsible for your life, the direction your life goes in and the outcomes you wish to achieve. No one else can be held responsible for your outcomes. When things do not go the way you had planned or expected, rather than blame anyone else, identify what went wrong and take responsibility for adjusting and getting back on track.

TIP 58: Overcome procrastination

Procrastination normally happens when you are unclear about why you are doing something, when you are unclear about how to achieve something, when you are not 100% committed to something or when you are fearful of the outcome (which can be success or failure).

Procrastination will cause you to subconsciously prioritise other things before the things that will actually move you closer to your goal of aligning your career with your desired lifestyle.

Procrastination comes disguised as variety of distractions from suddenly having the urge to clear all the cupboards or your wardrobes to organising all your food tins into alphabetical order, to a friend or family crisis that you just must resolve. Procrastination also comes disguised as TV programmes, computer games, Internet surfing, Facebook, reading magazines, etc.

Become conscious of the things you are doing regularly that are not moving you towards your goal. Also, become more aware of things you start to do that you would not normally choose to do. Keep your vision board somewhere you can see it daily, and review your vision statement regularly in order to maintain motivation and to help overcome procrastination.

TIP 59: Be open-minded

Even if you have a clear plan of how you will align your career with your desired lifestyle, life can sometimes change things. Alternatively, you may have a clear vision for your desired lifestyle but you may be unsure of how you can achieve it. These are both obstacles that can tempt you to give up on your goal. This is why it is important to remain open-minded. Just because your plans do not happen exactly as you intended, this does not mean there is not another way to achieve the same or a similar outcome.

Equally, if you are unclear about how to achieve something, do not automatically dismiss an idea or opportunity you would ordinarily overlook, as you never know where it could lead. Ensure it is linked to your overall goal of aligning your career with your desired lifestyle in some way to ensure you can distinguish between an opportunity and a distraction. Being open-minded helps you to become more aware of the opportunities around you, increasing your chances of achieving your goal.

TIP 60: Leave your comfort zone

In order to achieve your goal of aligning your career with your desired lifestyle, you will have to leave your comfort zone. The reason you have not done so already is because you are scared to leave what you know and move into uncertainty.

Our comfort zone is a nice place to be initially. It is a place we are familiar with, where we feel safe and content. However, a prison is also a place of safety. It keeps society safe from offenders and keeps offenders safe from each other. However, it is not a place you would choose to spend your time. Over time your comfort zone can become like a prison. You know there is more to life and more you would like to achieve, but you have become so familiar with and content in your comfort zone that you are not motivated to leave it. Eventually, it starts to become **un**comfortable and that is when you start to feel frustrated and unfulfilled. You will also start to feel trapped because you are aware of what is happening, but you are too scared of the unknown to do anything about it. You need to move before you are ready. You need to leave your comfort zone before it becomes too uncomfortable. Start small, and do things that you are not necessarily familiar with, but that will move you closer to your goal.

TIP 61: Be patient

In today's society we have become used to everything happening instantly and, as a result, for anything we do in life we expect instant results. However, achieving a goal such as aligning your career with your desired lifestyle takes patience. There will times when everything is falling into place and happening exactly as you planned; times when you will feel focused, energised and motivated. There will also be times when you will feel the complete opposite: times when you will feel tired, frustrated and unclear. There will be tasks that you can do which will have immediate results, and there will also be actions you take that will take longer for the results to be seen.

It is important that you have patience and trust the process.

You have thought your plan through in detail, so just keep in mind the vision of your desired lifestyle. And remember: Nothing happens before it's time.

TIP 62: Act 'as if'

Nothing happens before it's time but there is no reason you cannot start to make small adjustments in alignment with your desired lifestyle. Many of us go through life acting as if what we want in life is impossible and will not happen, so, of course, that is exactly what happens: nothing.

***You need to act as if everything you want to
achieve is already a reality.***

When you start to act as if your desired lifestyle is already a
reality, you attach feelings and emotions to your vision
which will make you want it more and will motivate you to
continue working towards your goal, overcoming any
obstacles and challenges you may encounter.

Acting as if your desired life is already a reality will alter
your mindset and you will start to think differently. This will
help open up your mind to new possibilities and
opportunities, and will in turn introduce you to a new
network of people who may be able to support your
transition from your current lifestyle to your desired
lifestyle. Acting 'as if' will also increase your belief that your
vision for your desired life can in fact become a reality.

TIP 63: Avoid comparing yourself to others

Once you start to act 'as if', you will start to become more
aware of people around you who have already achieved the
lifestyle you desire. It can be very tempting to look at these
people and make judgements about them and yourself. You
may tell yourself that they had more money, time, support
or knowledge than you when they started out, which is why
they were able to achieve the lifestyle you desire. You may
also be tempted to compare your progress to their
progress. You may tell yourself that they have made so
much more progress than you or that you are not doing as
well as them. It is important to remember that everyone
starts from a different place in life with different
circumstances and different resources available to them.

It is very useful to look at people who have already
achieved the lifestyle you desire in order to learn from their
mistakes, failures and successes and to gain inspiration and
motivation from their journey. However, do not compare

yourself to them as, no matter how similar your journey may seem, it is almost certain that there will be factors that are different. Comparing yourself to others for the purpose of telling yourself how badly you are doing is a waste of energy that could be better spent working towards achieving your goal.

TIP 64: Reward yourself

It is important not only to recognise the progress you make but also to reward yourself. It takes a lot of courage and commitment to take on a journey such as aligning your career with your desired lifestyle. It also takes a lot of hard work and dedication, and there will be some very challenging times. For this reason, it is important to reward your efforts so that you do not feel like all your efforts are in vain, especially if your desired lifestyle will take a lot of your time and energy to achieve.

It can be tempting to delay any form of reward until you achieve your overall goal. However, you will need a lot of motivation along the way, and rewarding yourself will not only force you to recognise how far you have come but will also act as motivation to continue on your journey. Build in a reward after each significant milestone and achievement in order to ensure that you acknowledge your progress.

TIP 65: Focus on the end goal

During your journey of aligning your career with your desired lifestyle, you will come across many distractions, obstacles and challenges, which are all part of the process. However, they can also tempt you to give up on your overall goal. At the same time, it is easy to get caught up with all the other things you have happening in your life and forget what you are working towards, how much you want what you are working towards, and why.

It is absolutely essential that you focus on the end goal and keep it in mind at all times.

You need a constant reminder of what you are working towards, and why. Your vision board and vision statement provide this reminder for you. Acting 'as if' also reminds you of what you are working towards. Every day, prioritise your tasks and ensure you do at least one thing that takes you closer to your goal. Ensure you are putting most of your time and effort into the tasks that will move you closer to your end goal.

TIP 66: Enjoy the journey

Although it is important to focus on the end goal, it is also important that you enjoy the journey. When you really want something, it can be tempting to focus solely on the end goal and miss all the amazing opportunities and experiences you encounter along the way. Life does not stop while you are working towards your goals. The planet keeps turning and life goes on. There is nothing worse than achieving your goal but looking back resenting all the time and energy you invested, feeling as though you missed out on so much in order to achieve your end goal.

Make sure your life does not become consumed with achieving your end goal. Make time for the things and people that are important to you because I am guessing your desired lifestyle will also involve them. If you spend your time focusing solely on your end goal, you will risk alienating the people that matter most and end up living your desired lifestyle alone. So, unless that is part of your plan, I suggest that you continue to make time for them throughout your journey.

Finally, do not take yourself too seriously, and do not miss out on living life today for what you want in the future.

After all, tomorrow is not guaranteed, and all we can be certain of is this present moment. So, as important as it is to plan ahead and to think about the future, we must not do so at the expense of enjoying the present.

Notes:

Well done for getting this far! Take some time to work through the questions and exercises in this final **D.R.E.A.M™** step and use this page to make notes.

_____

_____

_____

_____

_____

_____

_____

_____

_____

_____

_____

_____

_____

_____

_____

_____

CONCLUSION

Now that you have worked through the sixty-six tips from **The D.R.E.A.M Project™** you should have a clear vision of your desired lifestyle, and it should be clear what you need to do to align your career with your vision. You should feel inspired and motivated to proactively take control of your career path and to create a life that is balanced and fulfilled.

If you are still saying you don't have the time, money or energy, you need to ask yourself: If not now, then when? And if not now, when and how will anything ever change?

How badly do you want to have this desired lifestyle?

On a scale of one to ten, where ten is you want this more than anything else you've ever wanted before, score how you are currently feeling. If it is lower than eight, ask yourself what needs to happen or change to increase your score.

The sixty-six tips contained in this book are practical tips that require no prior knowledge, skills or experience. Therefore, there is no reason you cannot start following them today. Happiness is something we all crave and spend our whole life either maintaining or searching for. My aim with this book is to bring you that bit closer to experiencing happiness on a daily basis, giving you tips that will enable you to create a life that is balanced and fulfilled.

I am very conscious of how tempting it will be to remain in your comfort zone and return to life as it was before you started reading this book. Therefore, continued support and resources are available via the website: www.llcoaching.co.uk

If you are one of those exceptional people who wants to align their career and desired lifestyle sooner rather than later, please get in touch at info@llcoaching.co.uk to find out about the empowering coaching programmes we have available to enable you to align you career and desired lifestyle **with velocity**.

Finally, I would love to hear about your experience of following the sixty-six tips from **The D.R.E.A.M Project™** and any progress you have made. Please keep in touch, and send any comments to feedback@llcoaching.co.uk

Good luck, and all the best.

Warmest wishes,

Leanne

www.ingramcontent.com/pod-product-compliance
Lightning Source LLC
Chambersburg PA
CBHW070028110426
42741CB00034B/2690